Encountering God

An Invitation to God's Word for Teenagers

Encountering God:
An Invitation to God's Word for Teenagers

©2015 by Edward R. Nasello
Proof Perfect Publishing

Additional copies of this book may be purchased at amazon.com.

If you would like to request a complimentary copy for someone who is unable to purchase this book, you may submit your request to eddie.jm@outlook.com.

Library of Congress Control Number: 2014960222

ISBN 10: 0-9831898-2-X
ISBN 13: 978-0-9831898-2-4

Don't let anyone look down on you because you are young, but set an example for the believers in speech, in conduct, in love, in faith and in purity.

1 Timothy 4:12 (NIV)

Table of Contents

Introduction

The book sat upon the shelf collecting dust, like an old trophy on display. Beneath the layer of dust, the cover looked as new as the day it was given to me by my grandmother. A close look at the pages, however, revealed some signs of aging as they had begun to turn yellow. The book of which I speak, of course, is my first Bible.

For many years, the Bible has traveled with me wherever I have gone. But until only a few years ago, it was rarely read.

Yes, I attended church weekly, believed in God, and prayed often. Still, though I did not admit it to myself at the time, I was always keeping God at arm's length away—close enough so He was there whenever I needed Him, but far enough away that I did not have to confront any demands that I feared might be placed on me if I chose to follow too closely.

On occasion, I would open the Bible and look down at the date inscribed on the first page by my grandmother— March 12, 1979. I would look at her handwriting and instantly be transported in my mind back to the day she gave me the Bible. My grandmother was an amazing person of faith who greatly influenced my understanding of what it means to be alive in Christ. She taught me that it is not enough to simply believe in God—we must encounter and come to know God.

For as long as I knew my grandmother, she always seemed to be at peace with everything—even when she lost her husband. Yes, she was saddened by her loss, but she clearly had a confidence that she would be with him again someday. For many years, I enjoyed talking with my grandmother about God, faith, and religion. Though these conversations did take root, they did not bear much fruit until later in my life.

I can still clearly recall sitting at my grandmother's bedside at the hospital late one night many years ago. By this point in time, she was growing old and spent much of her time in hospital beds recovering from surgery. On this particular occasion, I remember thinking to myself that she would not be coming home again. I knew it, and so did she. We talked for almost an hour, when I finally mustered up the courage and blurted out, "Are you afraid?"

Knowing exactly what I was asking, my grandmother's smile grew even bigger as she proceeded to tell me that she had lived a good life and was looking forward to being with her husband again. "I am ready," she declared in a resolute manner.

A few weeks later, my grandmother passed away. The words *I am ready* continued to echo in my mind. What about me, I thought, am I ready? What do I need to do to be ready? How can I experience the joy and peace my grandmother so clearly felt even in the face of death?

My mind was flooded with questions. But like so many times before, I allowed the distractions of life to steer me off course, leaving these questions unanswered. Like a stubborn driver, I gripped the wheel tightly and kept God in the passenger seat.

Then one morning, I walked into my office and sat in front of the computer, waiting for it to boot up. I turned and looked out the window to say a prayer to start my day. I had performed this morning ritual every day for as long as I could remember, but this time something was different. Never before and never since have I ever felt such a strong sense of being in the presence of God. Not only could I feel God around me, but also I could feel God inside of me.

When I shared this story with an acquaintance of mine whom I had not seen in years, he declared, "Know what I think? ... God has just tapped you on the shoulder." I can think of no better explanation. Indeed, God did tap me on the shoulder. Though, I suspect it wasn't the first time, it was the first time that I took notice. And as I felt this new life that was breathed into me, I relented and let go of the wheel—it was now God's turn to drive.

That night, as I got ready for bed, I truly understood for the first time in my life what Jesus meant when He spoke about the need to be born again. I turned and picked up the Bible that sat on the shelf, brushed away the dust, and began to read—and I was indeed born again. I soon discovered answers to the questions that had lingered in my heart and head for so many years. But this new wisdom also gave birth to even more questions. In time, I learned that the questions conceived when reading the Bible are just as important as the answers that are revealed. It is precisely the questions we ask that help us to build a relationship with God. These questions lead us to evaluate the choices we make in light of truth and wisdom that draw us closer to God. Each time we discover an answer, a new question arises. It is like following a trail of breadcrumbs that leads to God.

When I think back to how many times I looked at my Bible sitting on the shelf without ever opening it to read, I can't help but to think how many other Bibles still sit unopened on shelves. How many people are still waiting to accept their invitation to encounter God through His Word?

Yes, God invites us to know Him intimately. He wants us to walk with Him every minute of every day. But to do this requires a commitment on our part. Our relationship with God will only thrive if we hold ourselves accountable for doing our part. We must work to strengthen this relationship each day, just as we would any other relationship. One way that we can do this is to commit ourselves to studying His word. If we want to know God, we must know the Bible.

No other book can be a substitute for the Bible—and certainly not this book. If you have not yet read the Bible, it is my sincerest hope that the pages that follow will help inspire you to dedicate yourself to exploring the Word of God so that you may come to know Him intimately. If you have already read the Bible, I pray that this book will lead you to a deeper understanding of God's Word through thoughtful reflection that strengthens your relationship with Him.

Just think, how often do we call out to God asking that He speak to us? He already has spoken—all we need to do is pick up a Bible and read what He has said.

– Chapter 1 –

GOD IS LOVE

It was late one night as I was reading the Bible. I was reading about God's love for us in 1 John 4. I almost missed it. In fact, I did miss it at first (or at least its importance). There in verse 16 were three words, stated as simply and directly as could be: *God is love*. I paused and read this sentence again. Could it be that simple? God is love?

I began to reflect carefully on the significance of these three words, when it occurred to me that maybe this was the answer to that most basic and fundamental question of all—"Why are we here?"

The Bible is filled with verses that tell of God's love for us and His urging us to love one another. But this simple statement in 1 John 4 is different. We are told that God *is* love. Perhaps these three words hold the key to understanding God's purpose in creating us.

Could it be that God created us simply so that His love would grow?

Think about it this way: Imagine one person, all alone in the world. How is it possible for that person's love to grow if there is no one else to love or to love this person back?

Now, imagine another person comes along. There is now someone to love and to love back. Love has grown. If the two people are joined together in marriage and have children, love increases yet again as the parents pour their love into their children and the children in turn pour their love into their parents.

Doesn't our relationship with God work the same way? If so, we can speculate that by creating us, God has satisfied a desire to make His love grow. What else do we

> **Think About It ...**
>
> Love doesn't have to be big. It can just be a simple little act of kindness.

possibly have to offer? After all, God is God—infinite and all-knowing, the Creator of heaven and Earth. Why would a God of infinite wisdom and power choose to create each of us, given our human frailties and imperfections? Perhaps, because first and foremost God is love. When God loves us and we love Him back, God's love grows. And when God's love grows,

God—who is love—in a sense also grows. Through this process, we who are invited to share in God's love are also invited to share in God. How cool is that!

The idea may be simple, but it is significant. God's love, through His relationship with us, is beyond measure, has no limits, and continues to grow.

God is love. But, do not simply take my word for it. This is a truth that you must discover for yourself. Read His words, know His love, and welcome God to walk with you as you lead a life that is a living testament to this great love.

1 JOHN 4:7-8 (NASB)

Beloved, let us love one another, for love is from God; and everyone who loves is born of God and knows God. The one who does not love does not know God, for God is love.

1 CORINTHIANS 13:4-7 (NIV)

Love is patient, love is kind. It does not envy, it does not boast, it is not proud. It does not dishonor others, it is not self-seeking, it is not easily angered, it keeps no record of wrongs. Love does not delight in evil but rejoices with the truth. It always protects, always trusts, always hopes, always perseveres.

ROMANS 8:38-39 (ESV)

For I am sure that neither death nor life, nor angels nor rulers, nor things present nor things to come, nor powers, nor height nor depth, nor anything else in all creation, will be able to separate us from the love of God in Christ Jesus our Lord.

ZEPHANIAH 3:17 (NLT)

For the LORD your God is living among you. He is a mighty savior. He will take delight in you with gladness. With his love, he will calm all your fears. He will rejoice over you with joyful songs.

JUDE 1:20-21 (NKJV)

But you, beloved, building yourselves up on your most holy faith, praying in the Holy Spirit, keep yourselves in the love of God, looking for the mercy of our Lord Jesus Christ unto eternal life.

JEREMIAH 31:3 (NIV)

The LORD appeared to us in the past, saying: "I have loved you with an everlasting love; I have drawn you with unfailing kindness."

1 JOHN 4:12 (NIV)

No one has ever seen God; but if we love one another, God lives in us and his love is made complete in us.

1 JOHN 4:16-19 (NLT)

We know how much God loves us, and we have put our trust in his love. God is love, and all who live in love live in God, and God lives in them. And as we live in God, our love grows more perfect. So we will not be afraid on the day of judgment, but we can face him with confidence because we live like Jesus here in this world. Such love has no fear, because perfect love expels all fear. If we are afraid, it is for fear of punishment, and this shows that we have not fully experienced his perfect love. We love each other because he loved us first.

LUKE 6:32-36 (WEB)

If you love those who love you, what credit is that to you? For even sinners love those who love them. If you do good to those who do good to you, what credit is that to you? For even sinners do the same. If you lend to those from whom you hope to receive, what credit is that to you? Even sinners lend to sinners, to receive back as much. But love your enemies, and do good, and lend, expecting nothing back; and your reward will be great, and you will be children of the Most High; for he is kind toward the unthankful and evil. Therefore be merciful, even as your Father is also merciful.

PSALM 103:11-12 (NLT)

For his unfailing love toward those who fear him is as great as the height of the heavens above the earth. He has removed our sins as far from us as the east is from the west.

1 JOHN 4:9-11 (NIV)

This is how God showed his love among us: He sent his one and only Son into the world that we might live through him. This is love: not that we loved God, but that he loved us and sent his Son as an atoning sacrifice for our sins. Dear friends, since God so loved us, we also ought to love one another.

PROVERBS 3:11-12 (NLT)

My child, don't reject the LORD'S discipline, and don't be upset when he corrects you. For the LORD corrects those he loves, just as a father corrects a child in whom he delights.

1 CORINTHIANS 13:1-3 (ESV)

If I speak in the tongues of men and of angels, but have not love, I am a noisy gong or a clanging cymbal. And if I have prophetic powers, and understand all mysteries and all knowledge, and if I have all faith, so as to remove mountains, but have not love, I am nothing. If I give away all I have, and if I deliver up my body to be burned, but have not love, I gain nothing.

1 JOHN 2:15-17 (ESV)

Do not love the world or the things in the world. If anyone loves the world, the love of the Father is not in him. For all that is in the world—the desires of the flesh and the desires of the eyes and pride of life—is not from the Father but is from the world. And the world is passing away along with its desires, but whoever does the will of God abides forever.

ROMANS 5:8 (NKJV)

But God demonstrates His own love toward us, in that while we were still sinners, Christ died for us.

DEUTERONOMY 7:9 (NLT)

Understand, therefore, that the LORD your God is indeed God. He is the faithful God who keeps his covenant for a thousand generations and lavishes his unfailing love on those who love him and obey his commands.

JOHN 3:16-17 (ESV)

For God so loved the world, that he gave his only Son, that whoever believes in him should not perish but have eternal life. For God did not send his Son into the world to condemn the world, but in order that the world might be saved through him.

EPHESIANS 3:14-18 (NLT)

When I think of all this, I fall to my knees and pray to the Father, the Creator of everything in heaven and on earth. I pray that from his glorious, unlimited resources he will empower you with inner strength through his Spirit. Then Christ will make his home in your hearts as you trust in him. Your roots will grow down into God's love and keep you strong. And may you have the power to understand, as all God's people should, how wide, how long, how high, and how deep his love is.

Prepare

Read 1 John 4:7-21 and answer the following questions:

Why do you think that John states "God is love"? What is the significance of this statement?

How is God's love made complete in us?

What has God done to show His love for you?

What have you done to show your love for God?

Perform

Acknowledge God's love for you each day. Make the time to reflect on all the ways that God demonstrates His love for you. Even during difficult times, God's love can be found. It may take greater effort on your part to see God's love during these times, but you can begin by reminding yourself that He gave His son to die so that you may share in the promise of eternal salvation.

> **Song for Reflection:** *Your Love Oh Lord* by Third Day
> *Available to watch and listen at **www.youtube.com**.*

Just For Fun

Scripture or Script—The Bible includes many messages about love; so do some of our favorite movies. Which of the following are Bible verses? Which of the following are lines from popular movies?

And now these three remain: faith, hope and love. But the greatest of these is love.

To love another person is to see the face of God.

Hatred stirs up conflict, but love covers over all wrongs.

The best love is the kind that awakens the soul and makes us reach for more, that plants a fire in our hearts and brings peace to our minds.

Death cannot stop true love. All it can do is delay it for a while.

Many waters cannot quench love; rivers cannot wash it away. If one were to give all the wealth of one's house for love, it would be utterly scorned.

– Chapter 2 –

LEAN ON HIM

Do you believe in God?

Wait—before you answer too quickly, think about what it means to *believe* in God. Think about what God is asking when He calls each one of us to believe in Him.

Does believing in God simply mean to acknowledge His existence? Keep in mind that even the devil himself acknowledges the existence of God.

Sadly, for too many people, this is the limit of their belief—to acknowledge the existence of God. Yet, the belief that God speaks of in the Bible goes far beyond just acknowledging His existence. It requires action on our part. When God calls us to believe in Him, He is asking that we "rely on Him" and "place our trust in Him." God wants us to lean on Him. This is how we demonstrate our belief in Him.

So, do you believe in God—completely and totally, or only up until a certain point? What do your actions say?

I can remember a time when I was a young child and my grandfather took me to the beach. I remember holding his hand and walking on the sand. I was at peace, and I was content in the moment. I was happy to be with my grandfather and to hold his hand as we walked together. I felt safe and secure and I did not want to let go of my grandfather's hand.

Then, something happened. My grandfather led me out into the ocean. As the water washed over my feet, I looked out and saw the vast ocean. I watched as wave after wave formed in the distance and grew in size as they approached the shore where I was standing. I heard the thunderous sound of each wave as they collapsed and the white foam rushed toward me. I wanted to turn back and run to the warm sand where

> ## Think About It ...
>
> How we respond to difficult circumstances reveals if our faith in God is genuine or if our prayers are just empty words.

it was safe—where it was calm and peaceful. But my grandfather picked me up and held me tight in his arms. He began to walk toward the waves, and I could feel my muscles tighten as a nervous tension began to well up inside of me. I tried to reassure myself that everything would be all right, as I looked at the other children who were out in the deep water laughing and having a good time. The ocean was calm in the deep water beyond the waves.

Surely, I thought, my grandfather would not let anything bad happen to me. We just need to get past the waves. Soon I would be laughing and playing with the other children, I told myself. Soon the waves that appeared before me would be behind me, and my fears would be washed away.

Then, the first wave hit and panic set in. I began to scream and cry. My grandfather continued to hold me tight and began to speak to me in a calm voice. But, I was too panic-stricken to understand a word he was saying. I began to squirm and tried to free myself from his protective embrace. I stretched my arms toward the beach and kicked violently with my feet as I struggled to break free.

Unwilling to give my trust completely to my grandfather, I continued to protest against his desire to lead me into deeper waters—until, at last, he relented and led me back to the shore. And with my feet again firmly planted on the warm sand, I did not hesitate to reach for my grandfather's hand. And he did not hesitate to let me place my hand in his.

But, what if I had only given my trust completely to my grandfather? I could have conquered my fears. I could have been out in the deep water with the other children who were laughing and having a good time. All I really needed to do was just lean on him and let him do the rest.

There are times in our lives when God asks each of us to step outside our comfort zone. These are the times that we need Him most. We do not need to go it alone—nor does He expect us to go it alone. Through His Word, God reminds us that when we need Him most, He will be there for us and will carry us safely past the waves into deeper waters—fully immersed in His love. All we need to do is lean on Him. When we can do that, then we will know we truly do believe in God.

PROVERBS 3:5-6 (ESV)

Trust in the LORD with all your heart, and do not lean on your own understanding. In all your ways acknowledge him, and he will make straight your paths.

JEREMIAH 17:7-8 (NIV)

But blessed is the one who trusts in the LORD, whose confidence is in him. They will be like a tree planted by the water that sends out its roots by the stream. It does not fear when heat comes; its leaves are always green. It has no worries in a year of drought and never fails to bear fruit.

PSALM 40:1-3 (NLT)

I waited patiently for the LORD to help me, and he turned to me and heard my cry. He lifted me out of the pit of despair, out of the mud and the mire. He set my feet on solid ground and steadied me as I walked along. He has given me a new song to sing, a hymn of praise to our God. Many will see what he has done and be amazed. They will put their trust in the LORD.

ISAIAH 40:28-31 (ESV)

Have you not known? Have you not heard? The LORD is the everlasting God, the Creator of the ends of the earth. He does not faint or grow weary; his understanding is unsearchable. He gives power to the faint, and to him who has no might he increases strength. Even youths shall faint and be weary, and young men shall fall exhausted; but they who wait for the LORD shall renew their strength; they shall mount up with wings like eagles; they shall run and not be weary; they shall walk and not faint.

PSALM 37:39-40 (ESV)

The salvation of the righteous is from the LORD; he is their stronghold in the time of trouble. The LORD helps them and delivers them; he delivers them from the wicked and saves them, because they take refuge in him.

ROMANS 12:12 (NIV)

Be joyful in hope, patient in affliction, faithful in prayer.

LUKE 11:9-10 (NLT)

And so I tell you, keep on asking, and you will receive what you ask for. Keep on seeking, and you will find. Keep on knocking, and the door will be opened to you. For everyone who asks, receives. Everyone who seeks, finds. And to everyone who knocks, the door will be opened.

PSALM 143:10-11 (NIV)

Teach me to do your will, for you are my God; may your good Spirit lead me on level ground. For your name's sake, LORD, preserve my life; in your righteousness, bring me out of trouble.

2 CORINTHIANS 12:9-10 (ESV)

But he said to me, "My grace is sufficient for you, for my power is made perfect in weakness." Therefore I will boast all the more gladly of my weaknesses, so that the power of Christ may rest upon me. For the sake of Christ, then, I am content with weaknesses, insults, hardships, persecutions, and calamities. For when I am weak, then I am strong.

PHILIPPIANS 4:6-7 (WEB)

In nothing be anxious, but in everything, by prayer and petition with thanksgiving, let your requests be made known to God. And the peace of God, which surpasses all understanding, will guard your hearts and your thoughts in Christ Jesus.

PSALM 25:4-5 (HCSB)

Make Your ways known to me, LORD; teach me Your paths. Guide me in Your truth and teach me, for You are the God of my salvation; I wait for You all day long.

JAMES 1:5-8 (NLT)

If you need wisdom, ask our generous God, and he will give it to you. He will not rebuke you for asking. But when you ask him, be sure that your faith is in God alone. Do not waver, for a person with divided loyalty is as unsettled as a wave of the sea that is blown and tossed by the wind. Such people should not expect to receive anything from the Lord. Their loyalty is divided between God and the world, and they are unstable in everything they do.

PSALM 121:1-2 (HCSB)

I lift my eyes toward the mountains. Where will my help come from? My help comes from the LORD, the Maker of heaven and earth.

MATTHEW 6:25-27 (WEB)

Therefore, I tell you, don't be anxious for your life: what you will eat, or what you will drink; nor yet for your body, what you will wear. Isn't life more than food, and the body more than clothing? See the birds of the sky, that they don't sow, neither do they reap, nor gather into barns. Your heavenly Father feeds them. Aren't you of much more value than they? Which of you, by being anxious, can add one moment to his lifespan?

JOSHUA 1:9 (ESV)

Have I not commanded you? Be strong and courageous. Do not be frightened, and do not be dismayed, for the LORD your God is with you wherever you go.

NAHUM 1:7 (HCSB)

The LORD is good, a stronghold in a day of distress;
He cares for those who take refuge in Him.

1 CORINTHIANS 10:13 (HCSB)

No temptation has overtaken you except what is common
to humanity. God is faithful, and He will not allow you to
be tempted beyond what you are able, but with the
temptation He will also provide a way of escape so that
you are able to bear it.

PSALM 139:23-24 (WEB)

Search me, God, and know my heart. Try me, and know
my thoughts. See if there is any wicked way in me, and
lead me in the everlasting way.

ISAIAH 41:13 (NLT)

For I hold you by your right hand—I, the LORD your God.
And I say to you, "Don't be afraid. I am here to
help you."

PHILIPPIANS 4:11-13 (WEB)

Not that I speak in respect to lack, for I have learned in whatever state I am, to be content in it. I know how to be humbled, and I know also how to abound. In everything and in all things I have learned the secret both to be filled and to be hungry, both to abound and to be in need. I can do all things through Christ, who strengthens me.

PSALM 51:10-12 (AMP)

Create in me a clean heart, O God, and renew a right, persevering, *and* steadfast spirit within me. Cast me not away from Your presence and take not Your Holy Spirit from me. Restore to me the joy of Your salvation and uphold me with a willing spirit.

JOB 22:21-22 (NIV)

Submit to God and be at peace with him; in this way prosperity will come to you. Accept instruction from his mouth and lay up his words in your heart.

ISAIAH 43:2 (NKJV)

When you pass through the waters, I *will be* with you;
And through the rivers, they shall not overflow you.
When you walk through the fire, you shall not be burned,
Nor shall the flame scorch you.

1 PETER 5:6-7 (WEB)

Humble yourselves therefore under the mighty hand of
God, that he may exalt you in due time; casting all your
worries on him, because he cares for you.

PSALM 37:23-24 (NLT)

The LORD directs the steps of the godly. He delights in
every detail of their lives. Though they stumble, they will
never fall, for the LORD holds them by the hand.

1 CORINTHIANS 1:25 (NIV)

For the foolishness of God is wiser than human wisdom,
and the weakness of God is stronger than human strength.

PSALM 34:17-19 (HCSB)

The righteous cry out, and the LORD hears, and delivers them from all their troubles. The LORD is near the brokenhearted; He saves those crushed in spirit. Many adversities come to the one who is righteous, but the LORD delivers him from them all.

JEREMIAH 29:12-13 (NKJV)

Then you will call upon Me and go and pray to Me, and I will listen to you. And you will seek Me and find *Me*, when you search for Me with all your heart.

Prepare

Read Luke 5:1-11 and answer the following questions:

Were the apostles certain of the outcome when they listened to Jesus and took their boat out into the deep water to cast their nets?

Did the apostles act based on what they wanted to do or what Jesus asked them to do?

Why did the apostles do what Jesus asked?

How were the lives of the apostles changed by this experience?

Perform

Look for opportunities each day to show trust in God. Identify the gifts and abilities God has blessed you with. Use these gifts and abilities to serve God, even when it means you must step outside your comfort zone. Lean on God through Scripture and prayer.

> **Song for Reflection:** *Need You Now* by Plumb
> *Available to watch and listen at www.youtube.com.*

Just For Fun

There are many people mentioned in the Bible who trusted God during difficult times. Read the clues below and name the people who had faith to lean on God.

I lost my wealth, family, and health, but after acknowledging my limitations and placing my trust in God, all was restored to me and I prospered.

I was sold into slavery by my brothers, but I never lost faith in God. I was reunited with my brothers and saved them from suffering during a famine.

Our brother became sick and died, but when we sent word to Jesus and asked for His help, He raised our brother from the dead.

When confronted by many enemies, I placed my trust in God and he helped me to lead the people of Israel to the Promised Land.

Because I refused to stop praying to God, I was thrown to the lions, but God sent an angel to protect me.

Chapter 3

The Invitation

Imagine you are planning a big party for a special occasion—a birthday or a graduation. You want all the people who are most important to you to share in celebrating this special occasion. Who will you invite? Who do you want to be at your side when the big day arrives? Who will get to share in the joy of celebrating with you? You must choose.

You think about all the people you know and how each person is special to you in a different way. Then, you start to make a list.

As you begin to write the names of the people you would like to invite, you realize that some will accept your invitation and some will not. You wish everyone would come, but you know that some people will make other plans. They will simply place your invitation aside.

Others, however, will respond enthusiastically to your invitation and eagerly wait for the big day to arrive.

Those who do come to your party will be greeted with a warm smile and a big hug. You will welcome them into your house. Each person who accepts your invitation honors you with his or her presence. Each person is grateful to have been invited.

Truly, invitations are wonderful things. They let us know that we have been chosen to take part in a special event or celebration. They affirm in us a sense of belonging. They provide us with an opportunity to present gifts to others.

> **Think About It ...**
>
> Live now as you will wish you had lived when you stand before God.

When Jesus came into this world, He was sent to us as an invitation. Through Jesus Christ, we are all invited to stand in the presence of God and share in His eternal glory. We have been chosen to enter the house of our Lord, to present our gifts to Him, and to honor Him through the lives that we live. We accept this invitation by accepting Jesus as our Lord and Savior.

Yes, you have been chosen. You have been invited. You have many gifts to offer. You have been called to walk with Jesus. The door to His kingdom has been placed in front of you. All you need to do is accept God's invitation and the door will be opened. You will walk into His loving embrace, He will rejoice at your presence, and the celebration will begin.

Many words have been used to describe Jesus: savior, lord, messiah, king, and teacher—just to name a few. But perhaps *invitation* is the word that describes Jesus best. Through the life of Jesus, we are invited to live by His example. Through the death of Jesus, we are invited to receive the grace of God and the forgiveness of our sins. Through the resurrection of Jesus, we are invited to enter God's heavenly kingdom.

Jesus is indeed an invitation sent to us from God. But unlike an invitation that comes in the mail and is placed aside after it has been read, Jesus is an invitation that remains with us always. We read this invitation each time that we open the Bible. We accept this invitation when we follow where Jesus leads us.

JOHN 4:14 (KJV)

But whosoever drinketh of the water that I shall give him shall never thirst; but the water that I shall give him shall be in him a well of water springing up into everlasting life.

1 CORINTHIANS 3:16 (ESV)

Do you not know that you are God's temple and that God's Spirit dwells in you?

ROMANS 8:29-30 (NIV)

For those God foreknew he also predestined to be conformed to the image of his Son, that he might be the firstborn among many brothers and sisters. And those he predestined, he also called; those he called, he also justified; those he justified, he also glorified.

REVELATION 3:20 (NASB)

Behold, I stand at the door and knock; if anyone hears My voice and opens the door, I will come in to him and will dine with him, and he with Me.

COLOSSIANS 3:23-24 (NIV)

Whatever you do, work at it with all your heart, as working for the Lord, not for human masters, since you know that you will receive an inheritance from the Lord as a reward. It is the Lord Christ you are serving.

JOHN 15:5-8 (NIV)

I am the vine; you are the branches. If you remain in me and I in you, you will bear much fruit; apart from me you can do nothing. If you do not remain in me, you are like a branch that is thrown away and withers; such branches are picked up, thrown into the fire and burned. If you remain in me and my words remain in you, ask whatever you wish, and it will be done for you. This is to my Father's glory, that you bear much fruit, showing yourselves to be my disciples.

2 CORINTHIANS 9:6-7 (WEB)

Remember this: he who sows sparingly will also reap sparingly. He who sows bountifully will also reap bountifully. Let each man give according as he has determined in his heart; not grudgingly, or under compulsion; for God loves a cheerful giver.

GALATIANS 2:20 (ESV)

I have been crucified with Christ. It is no longer I who live, but Christ who lives in me. And the life I now live in the flesh I live by faith in the Son of God, who loved me and gave himself for me.

ROMANS 12:2 (WEB)

Don't be conformed to this world, but be transformed by the renewing of your mind, so that you may prove what is the good, well-pleasing, and perfect will of God.

ACTS 20:24 (NLT)

But my life is worth nothing to me unless I use it for finishing the work assigned me by the Lord Jesus— the work of telling others the Good News about the wonderful grace of God.

JAMES 2:26 (NASB)

For just as the body without *the* spirit is dead, so also faith without works is dead.

EPHESIANS 2:10 (NIV)

For we are God's handiwork, created in Christ Jesus to do good works, which God prepared in advance for us to do.

2 TIMOTHY 1:9 (HCSB)

He has saved us and called us with a holy calling, not according to our works, but according to His own purpose and grace, which was given to us in Christ Jesus before time began.

GALATIANS 1:10 (NIV)

Am I now trying to win the approval of human beings, or of God? Or am I trying to please people? If I were still trying to please people, I would not be a servant of Christ.

ROMANS 8:28 (HCSB)

We know that all things work together for the good of those who love God: those who are called according to His purpose.

MATTHEW 16:24-27 (NIV)

Then Jesus said to his disciples, "Whoever wants to be my disciple must deny themselves and take up their cross and follow me. For whoever wants to save their life will lose it, but whoever loses their life for me will find it. What good will it be for someone to gain the whole world, yet forfeit their soul? Or what can anyone give in exchange for their soul? For the Son of Man is going to come in his Father's glory with his angels, and then he will reward each person according to what they have done."

JOHN 15:15-16 (WEB)

No longer do I call you servants, for the servant doesn't know what his lord does. But I have called you friends, for everything that I heard from my Father, I have made known to you. You didn't choose me, but I chose you, and appointed you, that you should go and bear fruit, and that your fruit should remain; that whatever you will ask of the Father in my name, he may give it to you.

HEBREWS 12:1-2 (HCSB)

Therefore, since we also have such a large cloud of witnesses surrounding us, let us lay aside every weight and the sin that so easily ensnares us. Let us run with endurance the race that lies before us, keeping our eyes on Jesus, the source and perfecter of our faith, who for the joy that lay before Him endured a cross and despised the shame and has sat down at the right hand of God's throne.

LUKE 11:33-36 (ESV)

No one after lighting a lamp puts it in a cellar or under a basket, but on a stand, so that those who enter may see the light. Your eye is the lamp of your body. When your eye is healthy, your whole body is full of light, but when it is bad, your body is full of darkness. Therefore be careful lest the light in you be darkness. If then your whole body is full of light, having no part dark, it will be wholly bright, as when a lamp with its rays gives you light.

MATTHEW 28:19-20 (ESV)

Go therefore and make disciples of all nations, baptizing them in the name of the Father and of the Son and of the Holy Spirit, teaching them to observe all that I have commanded you. And behold, I am with you always, to the end of the age.

1 PETER 3:13-17 (NLT)

Now, who will want to harm you if you are eager to do good? But even if you suffer for doing what is right, God will reward you for it. So don't worry or be afraid of their threats. Instead, you must worship Christ as Lord of your life. And if someone asks about your hope as a believer, always be ready to explain it. But do this in a gentle and respectful way. Keep your conscience clear. Then if people speak against you, they will be ashamed when they see what a good life you live because you belong to Christ. Remember, it is better to suffer for doing good, if that is what God wants, than to suffer for doing wrong!

DEUTERONOMY 14:2 (NKJV)

For you are a holy people to the LORD your God, and the Lord has chosen you to be a people for Himself, a special treasure above all the peoples who are on the face of the earth.

PHILIPPIANS 4:8-9 (WEB)

Finally, brothers, whatever things are true, whatever things are honorable, whatever things are just, whatever things are pure, whatever things are lovely, whatever things are of good report; if there is any virtue, and if there is any praise, think about these things. The things which you learned, received, heard, and saw in me: do these things, and the God of peace will be with you.

Prepare

Read John 4:1-30 and answer the following questions:

What is the symbolic meaning of the *well* and the *water* in this story?

What invitation does Jesus offer to the woman at the well?

What does Jesus mean when He tells the woman that whoever drinks the *living water* will never thirst again?

Does the woman at the well accept the invitation from Jesus? How do you know?

Perform

Accept Jesus' invitation to drink from the well of living water. Do not go through life relying on other people to quench your spiritual thirst—only God can do that. Strengthen your relationship with God through Jesus. Speak to Jesus and ask Him to speak to you, follow Him by following His example, and honor Him by honoring His Word.

> **Song for Reflection:** *The Well* by Casting Crowns
> *Available to watch and listen at **www.youtube.com**.*

Just For Fun

Each of the apostles received an invitation to follow Jesus. Read the clues below and see if you can name the apostles being described.

I was a tax collector named Levi when Jesus came and asked me to follow Him.

We were with Jesus on the mountain and witnessed His transfiguration.

When Jesus came to me on the road to Damascus, I was temporarily blinded.

I am Peter's brother and was fishing with him on the Sea of Galilee when Jesus asked us to become fishers of men.

The words *Zealot* and *Canaanite* have been used often to describe me.

I was chosen as the apostle to replace Judas.

I was filled with doubt when Jesus first appeared following His resurrection.

– Chapter 4 –

ONE BODY IN CHRIST

The apostle Paul reminds us that in Christ we are one body (Rom 12:5) and warns us not to think more highly of ourselves than we ought to (Rom 12:3). The message is simple, yet how we struggle to live by these words.

One of the many blessings that we have received from God is that He has made each one of us a unique person. We have each been given different gifts to use to serve the Lord. Clearly, this is by His design and He does not want nor expect us to be exactly the same. Therefore, it should be no surprise that there are so many different groups of people who identify themselves as Christians. What is somewhat surprising, however, is how many barriers we often place between one another. So much time is spent putting up walls when we should be building bridges.

Despite all of our differences, God loves us each the same. God has no favorites. He calls out to the world and does not cast anyone aside. He asks that we do the same.

Yes, we must always be on guard against negative influences in our lives and remain faithful to the Word of God, but we must be equally vigilant not to become so rigid in our way of thinking that we limit ourselves to only interacting with others who think exactly like us. We should not limit our faith journey to one building or one group of people. When we limit ourselves in this way, we begin to think of one another in terms of *us* and *them* when we should be thinking of one another as brothers and sisters in Christ.

> ## Think About It ...
>
> Do not think of yourself as a pond. Instead, see yourself as part of a river.

There is too much division and unrest in this world. There is too much pride and not enough humility. We must be confident enough to believe that we can teach one another, yet we must remain humble enough to acknowledge that we can learn from one another as well. As Christians, we must set the example. We must live in unity by building on common ground. That common ground is Jesus. Through Jesus, we are called together to live as one body—a body with many parts, but still one body.

If we really want the world to know what it means to be Christian, we must demonstrate that despite our differences there is an unbreakable bond between us. We must show the world that it is our relationship with God—and by extension with one another—that defines who we really are.

Think about how much could be accomplished if all Christians were united in their commitment to doing God's work. Unfortunately, all too often, we allow our personal thoughts and feelings to get in the way of God's plan for us. Instead of embracing the idea that we are an important part of one body, we set ourselves apart from the body. We do this whenever we think more highly of ourselves than others. This is exactly what the apostle Paul warned us not to do. This not only leads us away from one another, but it also leads us away from Christ. We must humble ourselves and resist the temptation to play the role of judge—but instead be a witness. We must work together as believers in Christ and invite *all* to hear God's Word.

As human beings, it seems to be in our nature to give most of our attention to noticing the differences between one another while failing to acknowledge the similarities. This kind of thinking often leads to isolation and confrontation. It would serve us well to remember that we are all children of God; and although Jesus is the only way to God, there are many ways to Jesus.

The differences between us are small, while the similarities are great. We share so many of the same beliefs—Jesus Christ, His crucifixion, His resurrection, and His promise of eternal life.

God does not want us to be a solo act or part of a small ensemble. He wants us to be a symphony orchestra. In a symphony orchestra, there are many different families of instruments. Each family may perform a different melody, but together the melodies are woven to form a completely harmonious sound. It is the conductor who makes this possible. Although there are many different families of instruments and many different performers in an orchestra, there is only one conductor. Everyone in the orchestra relies on the same conductor and is guided to perform in perfect unison with one another.

God is our conductor. Like musicians in an orchestra, we must follow the lead of our Great Conductor. Apart we are but an unfinished symphony. Together we can create an awesome and beautiful sound for everyone to hear. We may even inspire others to join the symphony.

MATTHEW 5:43-44 (AMP)

You have heard that it was said, You shall love your neighbor and hate your enemy; But I tell you, Love your enemies and pray for those who persecute you.

ROMANS 12:14-16 (NIV)

Bless those who persecute you; bless and do not curse. Rejoice with those who rejoice; mourn with those who mourn. Live in harmony with one another. Do not be proud, but be willing to associate with people of low position. Do not be conceited.

GALATIANS 5:25-26 (NKJV)

If we live in the Spirit, let us also walk in the Spirit. Let us not become conceited, provoking one another, envying one another.

PSALM 133:1 (KJV)

Behold, how good and how pleasant it is for brethren to dwell together in unity!

GALATIANS 6:4-5 (NLT)

Pay careful attention to your own work, for then you will get the satisfaction of a job well done, and you won't need to compare yourself to anyone else. For we are each responsible for our own conduct.

ROMANS 12:17-21 (NASB)

Never pay back evil for evil to anyone. Respect what is right in the sight of all men. If possible, so far as it depends on you, be at peace with all men. Never take your own revenge, beloved, but leave room for the wrath *of God*, for it is written, "VENGEANCE IS MINE, I WILL REPAY," says the Lord. "BUT IF YOUR ENEMY IS HUNGRY, FEED HIM, AND IF HE IS THIRSTY, GIVE HIM A DRINK; FOR IN SO DOING YOU WILL HEAP BURNING COALS ON HIS HEAD." Do not be overcome by evil, but overcome evil with good.

1 CORINTHIANS 1:10 (NLT)

I appeal to you, dear brothers and sisters, by the authority of our Lord Jesus Christ, to live in harmony with each other. Let there be no divisions in the church. Rather, be of one mind, united in thought and purpose.

2 CORINTHIANS 1:3-5 (NLT)

All praise to God, the Father of our Lord Jesus Christ. God is our merciful Father and the source of all comfort. He comforts us in all our troubles so that we can comfort others. When they are troubled, we will be able to give them the same comfort God has given us. For the more we suffer for Christ, the more God will shower us with his comfort through Christ.

COLOSSIANS 3:12-15 (NLT)

Since God chose you to be the holy people he loves, you must clothe yourselves with tenderhearted mercy, kindness, humility, gentleness, and patience. Make allowance for each other's faults, and forgive anyone who offends you. Remember, the Lord forgave you, so you must forgive others. Above all, clothe yourselves with love, which binds us all together in perfect harmony. And let the peace that comes from Christ rule in your hearts. For as members of one body you are called to live in peace. And always be thankful.

HEBREWS 10:24-25 (NLT)

Let us think of ways to motivate one another to acts of love and good works. And let us not neglect our meeting together, as some people do, but encourage one another, especially now that the day of his return is drawing near.

GALATIANS 6:9-10 (HCSB)

So we must not get tired of doing good, for we will reap at the proper time if we don't give up. Therefore, as we have opportunity, we must work for the good of all, especially for those who belong to the household of faith.

PROVERBS 19:11 (ESV)

Good sense makes one slow to anger, and it is his glory to overlook an offense.

JAMES 5:9 (NIV)

Don't grumble against one another, brothers and sisters, or you will be judged. The Judge is standing at the door!

MATTHEW 6:14-15 (NIV)

For if you forgive other people when they sin against you, your heavenly Father will also forgive you. But if you do not forgive others their sins, your Father will not forgive your sins.

JAMES 5:16 (NIV)

Therefore confess your sins to each other and pray for each other so that you may be healed. The prayer of a righteous person is powerful and effective.

EPHESIANS 4:2-6 (NLT)

Always be humble and gentle. Be patient with each other, making allowance for each other's faults because of your love. Make every effort to keep yourselves united in the Spirit, binding yourselves together with peace. For there is one body and one Spirit, just as you have been called to one glorious hope for the future. There is one Lord, one faith, one baptism, one God and Father of all, who is over all, in all, and living through all.

1 CORINTHIANS 12:6 (NLT)

God works in different ways, but it is the same God who does the work in all of us.

PHILIPPIANS 2:3-4 (NIV)

Do nothing out of selfish ambition or vain conceit. Rather, in humility value others above yourselves, not looking to your own interests but each of you to the interests of the others.

MATTHEW 7:1-2 (NLT)

Do not judge others, and you will not be judged. For you will be treated as you treat others. The standard you use in judging is the standard by which you will be judged.

EPHESIANS 4:29 (NLT)

Don't use foul or abusive language. Let everything you say be good and helpful, so that your words will be an encouragement to those who hear them.

1 PETER 4:9-10 (HCSB)

Be hospitable to one another without complaining. Based on the gift each one has received, use it to serve others, as good managers of the varied grace of God.

COLOSSIANS 3:8-10 (NLT)

But now is the time to get rid of anger, rage, malicious behavior, slander, and dirty language. Don't lie to each other, for you have stripped off your old sinful nature and all its wicked deeds. Put on your new nature, and renewed as you learn to know your Creator and become like him.

PHILIPPIANS 2:14-15 (HCSB)

Do everything without grumbling and arguing, so that you may be blameless and pure, children of God who are faultless in a crooked and perverted generation, among whom you shine like stars in the world.

1 JOHN 1:7 (NKJV)

But if we walk in the light as He is in the light, we have fellowship with one another, and the blood of Jesus Christ His Son cleanses us from all sin.

1 CORINTHIANS 12:12-14 (NIV)

Just as a body, though one, has many parts, but all its many parts form one body, so it is with Christ. For we were all baptized by one Spirit so as to form one body—whether Jews or Gentiles, slave or free—and we were all given the one Spirit to drink. Even so the body is not made up of one part but of many.

EPHESIANS 4:16 (NLT)

He makes the whole body fit together perfectly. As each part does its own special work, it helps the other parts grow, so that the whole body is healthy and growing and full of love.

PROVERBS 17:17 (AMP)

A friend loves at all times, and is born, as is a brother, for adversity.

GALATIANS 6:2 (NIV)

Carry each other's burdens, and in this way you will fulfill the law of Christ.

COLOSSIANS 1:17 (NASB)

He is before all things, and in Him all things hold together.

JOHN 10:14-16 (HCSB)

I am the good shepherd. I know My own sheep, and they know Me, as the Father knows Me, and I know the Father. I lay down My life for the sheep. But I have other sheep that are not of this fold; I must bring them also, and they will listen to My voice. Then there will be one flock, one shepherd.

Prepare

Read Romans 12:3-8 and 1 Corinthians 12:12-31, and then answer the following questions:

Why does the apostle Paul refer to Christians as the *body* of Christ?

Is it better for all parts of the *body* to be different or the same? Explain why.

In Romans 12:7-8, the apostle Paul identifies different gifts that God has given each person. What gifts do you think you have been given?

Perform

Be an active member of your church community. First, look for ways to interact and work together with other members of your church. Then, look for ways to reach out beyond your church. Do not limit the work that you do for God to one place or one group of people. The *body* of Christ refers to all believers in Christ. Seek ways to bring people from different church communities together. Seek ways to make people from outside church communities feel welcome at your church.

Song for Reflection: *We Believe* by Newsboys
*Available to watch and listen at **www.youtube.com**.*

Just For Fun

Throughout the Bible, we see examples of how people are called to serve God in different ways. Look at the list of names below. Identify who were prophets, who were priests, and who were kings.

Solomon	Anna
Eleazor	Samuel
Ezekiel	Aaron
Miriam	David
Jehoshaphat	Deborah
Malachi	Jeremiah
Jehoiakim	Zadok
Melchizedek	John the Baptist
Nathan	Saul
Moses	Asa

– Chapter 5 –

The Best is Yet to Come

Every day is a blessing from our Lord. Still, there are some days that are full of so much pain and suffering, it is difficult for us to make sense of the world in which we live. We get stuck in the moment and lose sight of God's promise to us—the promise that the best is yet to come.

For those who believe, the day will come when there will be no more death, nor sorrow, nor pain. The former things of the world in which we now live will pass away. Though we can only live in the moment, there are times when we need to look beyond the moment to draw strength. But this is something that often proves to be easier said than done.

We have all experienced pain and suffering during our lives. We have all seen others who we care about deeply experience pain and suffering. We have been confronted by the loss of loved ones. If we are not careful, our faith in God can be shaken. If we focus only on the moment, we just see a snapshot of our existence—we do not see the whole picture and may begin to have doubts about God's plan for us.

Now, imagine for a moment that you could fast forward to that day when you will be called to stand in the presence of our Lord. Imagine that you could experience heaven with all of your senses and know beyond any shadow of a doubt what awaits you. Then, image being returned to this very moment in time. Think how your perspective on life would be changed.

> **Think About It** ...
>
> Life is not about being but becoming. The purpose of our journey is not to live a perfect life but to allow God to perfect us through the experiences of life.

The knowledge of the life yet to come would most assuredly make it easier to endure the pain and suffering that is sometimes experienced in this life. Even the thought of death would not seem so unbearable. You would have incontrovertible proof that death is not an ending. It is just one event on a journey that will bring you closer to God.

So, why doesn't God allow us to have a "sneak peak" at what awaits us?

Well, maybe if He did, we would all be in one big rush to begin our next life before completing the work we have been called to do in this life and miss out on experiencing the fullness of His joy that has been planned for us in the here and now. Or, maybe God is just allowing for us to grow in our faith.

Regardless of the reason, we already have what we need to sustain us on our journey—we have God's promise. Through His Word, we know that the day will come when there will be no more pain, no more suffering, no more sorrow, and no more death. Through His Word, we know that whoever believes in Him shall not perish but have everlasting life. Through His Word, we know that the best is yet to come!

JEREMIAH 29:11 (NIV)

"For I know the plans I have for you," declares the LORD, "plans to prosper you and not to harm you, plans to give you hope and a future."

HEBREWS 11:1 (KJV)

Now faith is the substance of things hoped for, the evidence of things not seen.

2 CORINTHIANS 4:17-18 (NIV)

For our light and momentary troubles are achieving for us an eternal glory that far outweighs them all. So we fix our eyes not on what is seen, but on what is unseen, since what is seen is temporary, but what is unseen is eternal.

COLOSSIANS 3:1-2 (NLT)

Since you have been raised to new life with Christ, set your sights on the realities of heaven, where Christ sits in the place of honor at God's right hand. Think about the things of heaven, not the things of earth.

PSALM 23:6 (NASB)

Surely goodness and lovingkindness will follow me all the days of my life, And I will dwell in the house of the LORD forever.

LUKE 6:37-38 (HCSB)

Do not judge, and you will not be judged. Do not condemn, and you will not be condemned. Forgive, and you will be forgiven. Give, and it will be given to you; a good measure—pressed down, shaken together, and running over—will be poured into your lap. For with the measure you use, it will be measured back to you.

HEBREWS 12:11 (ESV)

For the moment all discipline seems painful rather than pleasant, but later it yields the peaceful fruit of righteousness to those who have been trained by it.

PROVERBS 19:21 (NIV)

Many are the plans in a person's heart, but it is the LORD'S purpose that prevails.

MATTHEW 6:19-21 (NASB)

Do not store up for yourselves treasures on earth, where moth and rust destroy, and where thieves break in and steal. But store up for yourselves treasures in heaven, where neither moth nor rust destroys, and where thieves do not break in or steal; for where your treasure is, there your heart will be also.

2 PETER 3:9 (ESV)

The Lord is not slow to fulfill his promise as some count slowness, but is patient toward you, not wishing that any should perish, but that all should reach repentance.

JAMES 1:12 (NIV)

Blessed is the one who perseveres under trial because, having stood the test, that person will receive the crown of life that the Lord has promised to those who love him.

ISAIAH 62:3 (NIV)

You will be a crown of splendor in the LORD'S hand, a royal diadem in the hand of your God.

ISAIAH 43:18-19 (NIV)

Forget the former things; do not dwell on the past. See, I am doing a new thing! Now it springs up; do you not perceive it? I am making a way in the wilderness and streams in the wasteland.

2 CORINTHIANS 5:17 (WEB)

Therefore if anyone is in Christ, he is a new creation. The old things have passed away. Behold, all things have become new.

1 JOHN 3:1-3 (ESV)

See what kind of love the Father has given to us, that we should be called children of God; and so we are. The reason why the world does not know us is that it did not know him. Beloved, we are God's children now, and what we will be has not yet appeared; but we know that when he appears we shall be like him, because we shall see him as he is. And everyone who thus hopes in him purifies himself as he is pure.

PHILIPPIANS 1:6 (NLT)

And I am certain that God, who began the good work within you, will continue his work until it is finally finished on the day when Christ Jesus returns.

JOHN 14:1-3 (ESV)

Let not your hearts be troubled. Believe in God; believe also in me. In my Father's house are many rooms. If it were not so, would I have told you that I go to prepare a place for you? And if I go and prepare a place for you, I will come again and will take you to myself, that where I am you may be also.

1 CORINTHIANS 9:24 (NASB)

Do you not know that those who run in a race all run, but *only* one receives the prize? Run in such a way that you may win.

GALATIANS 5:5 (NLT)

But we who live by the Spirit eagerly wait to receive by faith the righteousness God has promised to us.

1 JOHN 2:24-25 (ESV)

Let what you heard from the beginning abide in you. If what you heard from the beginning abides in you, then you too will abide in the Son and in the Father. And this is the promise that he made to us—eternal life.

I CORINTHIANS 2:9 (KJV)

But as it is written, Eye hath not seen, nor ear heard, neither have entered into the heart of man, the things which God hath prepared for them that love him.

PSALM 116:15 (NIV)

Precious in the sight of the LORD is the death of his faithful servants.

REVELATION 21:4 (ESV)

He will wipe away every tear from their eyes, and death shall be no more, neither shall there be mourning, nor crying, nor pain anymore, for the former things have passed away.

Prepare

Read Matthew 5:1-12 and Revelation 21:1-8, and then answer the following questions:

In the Bible verses from Matthew, Chapter 5, who does Jesus offer encouragement to?

In the Bible verses from Revelation, Chapter 21, how is heaven described?

What promises are made to us in all of these Bible verses?

Do you often reflect on the promises God has made to you? What steps can you take to strengthen your faith in God and the promises He has made?

Perform

Reflect often on God's Word and His promises. Allow God to speak to you and reassure you about His plans for you by reading the Bible. Even though you may not be able to see past the moment, God can—and He wants what is best for you. Place your trust in God and rest in the knowledge that the best is truly yet to come.

> **Song for Reflection:** *I Will Rise* by Chris Tomlin
> *Available to watch and listen at www.youtube.com*

Just For Fun

Many events are described in the Bible before they ever happened. Name the book of the Bible where these prophesies can be found.

1. The Messiah would be a descendant of David:

"Behold, the days are coming," says the LORD, "That I will raise to David a Branch of righteousness; A King shall reign and prosper, And execute judgment and righteousness in the earth."

2. The Messiah would be born of a virgin:

Therefore the Lord himself will give you a sign. Behold, the virgin shall conceive and bear a son, and shall call his name Immanuel.

3. The Messiah would be born in Bethlehem:

But you, Bethlehem Ephrathah, … out of you shall come forth to Me The One to be Ruler in Israel, Whose goings forth are from of old, From everlasting.

4. The Messiah would suffer and rise from the dead:

And the Son of Man will be delivered over to the chief priests and scribes, and they will condemn him to death and deliver him over to the Gentiles to be mocked and flogged and crucified, and he will be raised on the third day.

– Chapter 6 –

LIVE BY HIS WORD

God has established a high set of standards for us to live by. He has done this not because He is a demanding God, but because He is a holy and loving God who knows what is best for us. He also knows that we are capable of so much more than we realize.

Every time we make a choice or choose a course of action, we define who we are. The question that each of us must ask is, "Am I living my life by God's standards or my own?"

If we are truly committed to living by God's set of standards, we must know what God asks and expects of us. We must allow ourselves to be influenced and shaped by God. We do this each time that we read the Bible and listen to His Word.

All of this begs one very important question ...

How often do you read the Bible?

Most Christians are very good when it comes to speaking to God. We pray all the time. But we are not always as good when it comes to listening to Him. A stronger commitment to reading the Bible is needed. Through the Bible, God is able to share with us His wisdom and His guidance. Other people can have a positive influence on our lives and share their thoughts about God's Word, but only the Bible *is* God's Word. If we want to be certain that we are living by God's standards, we must trust in the one true source of His Word—the Bible.

When I was younger, my favorite subject at school was history. In particular, I loved American history. Most of what I learned came from school textbooks and what teachers told me. By the time I graduated from high school, I thought I knew all that I needed to know. But as I got older, I began reading more books about American history. Many of the books I read included

> **Think About It ...**
>
> Which have you allowed to have a greater impact on your life—the culture you live in or the Word of God?

primary source information—letters written by George Washington and Thomas Jefferson; transcripts of speeches by John Adams and James Madison; and the complete text of important documents such as the Declaration of Independence and the United States Constitution. Reading these primary source documents was a truly eye-opening experience. I could not believe how much I learned that I did not previously know. Even more importantly, I knew that what I learned from these primary sources was reliable. The information was not edited, paraphrased, or distorted in any way by personal bias.

For the same reason it is important to read primary source documents if you wish to have an accurate understanding of history, it is important to read the Bible if you wish to have an accurate understanding of God's Word—it is the written source of this important information.

Yes, it takes a commitment to read the Bible. But, it is well worth the commitment.

I can remember the first time that I picked up a Bible to read it in its entirety. I must confess, I felt a bit overwhelmed. I remember thinking, "this is going to take forever to read." (Forever, as it turned out, was about one year.) I also remember how I struggled and became frustrated at times because I thought I would find the answers to all of my questions in the Bible—yet the more I read, the more questions I seemed to have.

Then one day I realized how important the questions were that I had begun asking. I realized how much God's Word was shaping the person I was becoming. The Bible was driving me to ask the questions that I needed to be asking and leading me closer and closer to becoming the person God wants me to be.

The first steps along any journey are often the most difficult to take. Many people don't read the Bible simply because they are afraid they will not understand it, or it will take too long to read, or it will require making changes in their lives that they do not want to make. Before reading the Bible for the first time, I experienced all of these feelings. But now I understand why the Bible is so important. It is more than just a book. It can change lives and save lost souls.

Inscribed on one of the pages in my Bible are the following words from Abraham Lincoln—

"Take all of this book upon reason that you can, and take the balance on faith, and you will live and die a happier and better man."

No truer words were ever spoken.

2 TIMOTHY 3:16-17 (NASB)

All Scripture is inspired by God and profitable for teaching, for reproof, for correction, for training in righteousness; so that the man of God may be adequate, equipped for every good work.

PSALM 19:7-8 (NASB)

The law of the LORD is perfect, restoring the soul; The testimony of the LORD is sure, making wise the simple. The precepts of the LORD are right, rejoicing the heart; The commandment of the LORD is pure, enlightening the eyes.

JAMES 1:22-24 (HCSB)

But be doers of the word and not hearers only, deceiving yourselves. Because if anyone is a hearer of the word and not a doer, he is like a man looking at his own face in a mirror. For he looks at himself, goes away, and immediately forgets what kind of man he was.

HEBREWS 4:12-13 (NKJV)

For the word of God *is* living and powerful, and sharper than any two-edged sword, piercing even to the division of soul and spirit, and of joints and marrow, and is a discerner of the thoughts and intents of the heart. And there is no creature hidden from His sight, but all things *are* naked and open to the eyes of Him to whom we *must give* account.

PSALM 119:27-28 (HCSB)

Help me understand the meaning of Your precepts so that I can meditate on Your wonders. I am weary from grief; strengthen me through Your word.

ISAIAH 40:8 (NIV)

The grass withers and the flowers fall, but the word of our God endures forever.

ROMANS 15:4 (ESV)

For whatever was written in former days was written for
our instruction, that through endurance and through the
encouragement of the Scriptures we might have hope.

2 SAMUEL 22:31 (NKJV)

As for God, His way *is* perfect; The word of the LORD *is*
proven; He *is* a shield to all who trust in Him.

PSALM 1:1-3 (NIV)

Blessed is the one who does not walk in step with the
wicked or stand in the way that sinners take or sit in the
company of mockers, but whose delight is in the law of
the LORD, and who meditates on his law day and night.
That person is like a tree planted by streams of water,
which yields its fruit in season and whose leaf does not
wither—whatever they do prospers.

1 JOHN 2:3-6 (NASB)

By this we know that we have come to know Him, if we keep His commandments. The one who says, "I have come to know Him," and does not keep His commandments, is a liar, and the truth is not in him; but whoever keeps His word, in him the love of God has truly been perfected. By this we know that we are in Him: the one who says he abides in Him ought himself to walk in the same manner as He walked.

JAMES 1:19-21 (NLT)

Understand this, my dear brothers and sisters: You must all be quick to listen, slow to speak, and slow to get angry. Human anger does not produce the righteousness God desires. So get rid of all the filth and evil in your lives, and humbly accept the word God has planted in your hearts, for it has the power to save your souls.

JOHN 1:1 (KJV)

In the beginning was the Word, and the Word was with God, and the Word was God.

ISAIAH 55:8-11 (NIV)

"For my thoughts are not your thoughts, neither are your ways my ways," declares the LORD. "As the heavens are higher than the earth, so are my ways higher than your ways and my thoughts than your thoughts. As the rain and the snow come down from heaven, and do not return to it without watering the earth and making it bud and flourish, so that it yields seed for the sower and bread for the eater, so is my word that goes out from my mouth: It will not return to me empty, but will accomplish what I desire and achieve the purpose for which I sent it."

PSALM 119:10-12 (NIV)

I seek you with all my heart; do not let me stray from your commands. I have hidden your word in my heart that I might not sin against you. Praise be to you, LORD; teach me your decrees.

LUKE 6:47-49 (NIV)

As for everyone who comes to me and hears my words and puts them into practice, I will show you what they are like. They are like a man building a house, who dug down deep and laid the foundation on rock. When a flood came, the torrent struck that house but could not shake it, because it was well built. But the one who hears my words and does not put them into practice is like a man who built a house on the ground without a foundation. The moment the torrent struck that house, it collapsed and its destruction was complete.

COLOSSIANS 3:16-17 (ESV)

Let the word of Christ dwell in you richly, teaching and admonishing one another in all wisdom, singing psalms and hymns and spiritual songs, with thankfulness in your hearts to God. And whatever you do, in word or deed, do everything in the name of the Lord Jesus, giving thanks to God the Father through him.

ROMANS 10:14 (ESV)

So faith comes from hearing, and hearing through the word of Christ.

1 PETER 1:23-25 (NLT)

For you have been born again, but not to a life that will quickly end. Your new life will last forever because it comes from the eternal, living word of God. As the Scriptures say,

"People are like grass; their beauty is like a flower in the field. The grass withers and the flower fades. But the word of the Lord remains forever."

And that word is the Good News that was preached to you.

Prepare

Read John 14:15-31 and answer the following questions:

How does Jesus say that we can show our love for Him?

What does Jesus say about anyone who does not obey, or keep, His words?

In addition to the Bible, what gift are we given to remind us of God's Word?

Perform

Make reading the Bible a priority in your life. Schedule time each day to read from the Bible. Then, rely on what you learn from reading the Bible to guide your actions. When you are confronted with difficult circumstances or decisions, seek direction from God. Think about what you know from reading the Bible and place your faith in God.

The Bible may not teach you how to become great, but it will teach you how to be good. Stay focused and keep your priorities in life straight—goodness is better than greatness.

Song for Reflection: *Word Of God Speak* by MercyMe
*Available to watch and listen at **www.youtube.com**.*

Just For Fun

How well do you know the Bible? See how many of the following Bible trivia questions you can answer correctly.

In what three languages was the Bible originally written?

Which books in the Bible are referred to as the Pentateuch?

How many verses are in the shortest chapter of the Bible?

What is the first book of the New Testament?

Which Gospels are referred to as the synoptic Gospels?

In which book of the Bible will you find the story of David and Goliath?

What are the city names of the seven churches mentioned in the Book of Revelation?

– Chapter 7 –

THANKS BE TO GOD

God has given us so much to be thankful for. He has given us all that we need to be the person that He calls each of us to be. Still, if you are like me, you probably have a tendency to devote more of your time in prayer to making requests than to giving thanks. It may take a little extra effort on our part, but we cannot afford to take for granted how much we have to be thankful for. Nor should we just limit our giving thanks to words only. When you stop to think about it, to *give* thanks requires taking action—otherwise we are just *saying* thanks.

While saying thanks may be a good start, it is the "giving" part that is most important. When we give thanks to God, we magnify His presence in the world. Giving thanks to God means to honor God with our actions. It means to acknowledge the gifts He has given us by using these gifts to live a life of service to God.

When we use our talents to help others, we are giving thanks to God. When we donate our time and our money to those who are in need, we are giving thanks to God. When we take the time out of each day to notice and appreciate the awe and wonder of the world around us, we are giving thanks to God.

Do not let a day pass without giving thanks to God. All that we have, we owe to our Creator. No blessing is too small that we should fail to give God our thanks.

Make giving thanks to God a habit. Make a conscious effort each day to acknowledge your blessings and to think about what you can do to honor God

Think About It …

What you are is God's gift to you. What you do is your gift to God.

through your actions. It may take some effort in the beginning, but if you stick with it, giving thanks will have important positive consequences in your life. It will strengthen your relationship with God and can lift your spirits during difficult times.

You may recall that during the last supper, as Jesus prepared for His death, He still took the time to give thanks. We must follow His example. Give thanks always—not just on days when things are going good, but especially on days when things are not going so good.

Taking the time to reflect on all the things you have to be thankful for is exactly what is needed during difficult times.

If you find there are some days when it is difficult to turn up reasons for giving thanks, just look to Scripture. It is a powerful reminder of how much you have to be thankful for—a loving and forgiving God who not only breathed you into life, but also offered up His only begotten son so that you may share in the promise of eternal life.

How truly blessed we are.

PSALM 92:1-2 (ESV)

It is good to give thanks to the LORD, to sing praises to your name, O Most High; to declare your steadfast love in the morning, and your faithfulness by night.

1 TIMOTHY 6:6-9 (NIV)

But godliness with contentment is great gain. For we brought nothing into the world, and we can take nothing out of it. But if we have food and clothing, we will be content with that. Those who want to get rich fall into temptation and a trap and into many foolish and harmful desires that plunge people into ruin and destruction.

2 CORINTHIANS 5:21 (NLT)

For God made Christ, who never sinned, to be the offering for our sin, so that we could be made right with God through Christ.

PSALM 100:3-5 (NIV)

Know that the LORD is God. It is he who made us, and we are his; we are his people, the sheep of his pasture. Enter his gates with thanksgiving and his courts with praise; give thanks to him and praise his name. For the LORD is good and his love endures forever; his faithfulness continues through all generations.

LUKE 15:4-7 (ESV)

What man of you, having a hundred sheep, if he has lost one of them, does not leave the ninety-nine in the open country, and go after the one that is lost, until he finds it? And when he has found it, he lays it on his shoulders, rejoicing. And when he comes home, he calls together his friends and his neighbors, saying to them, "Rejoice with me, for I have found my sheep that was lost." Just so, I tell you, there will be more joy in heaven over one sinner who repents than over ninety-nine righteous persons who need no repentance.

JOHN 3:16-17 (ESV)

For God so loved the world, that he gave his only Son, that whoever believes in him should not perish but have eternal life. For God did not send his Son into the world to condemn the world, but in order that the world might be saved through him.

ISAIAH 53:5-6 (NIV)

But he was pierced for our transgressions, he was crushed for our iniquities; the punishment that brought us peace was on him, and by his wounds we are healed. We all, like sheep, have gone astray, each of us has turned to our own way; and the LORD has laid on him the iniquity of us all.

1 CORINTHIANS 1:18 (NIV)

For the message of the cross is foolishness to those who are perishing, but to us who are being saved it is the power of God.

ROMANS 10:9-11 (HCSB)

If you confess with your mouth, "Jesus is Lord," and believe in your heart that God raised Him from the dead, you will be saved. One believes with the heart, resulting in righteousness, and one confesses with the mouth, resulting in salvation. Now the Scripture says, Everyone who believes on Him will not be put to shame.

ROMANS 3:23-26 (NLT)

For everyone has sinned; we all fall short of God's glorious standard. Yet God freely and graciously declares that we are righteous. He did this through Christ Jesus when he freed us from the penalty for our sins. For God presented Jesus as the sacrifice for sin. People are made right with God when they believe that Jesus sacrificed his life, shedding his blood. This sacrifice shows that God was being fair when he held back and did not punish those who sinned in times past, for he was looking ahead and including them in what he would do in this present time. God did this to demonstrate his righteousness, for he himself is fair and just, and he declares sinners to be right in his sight when they believe in Jesus.

TITUS 3:4-7 (HCSB)

But when the kindness of God our Savior and His love for mankind appeared, He saved us—not by works of righteousness that we had done, but according to His mercy, through the washing of regeneration and renewal by the Holy Spirit. He poured out this Spirit on us abundantly through Jesus Christ our Savior, so that having been justified by His grace, we may become heirs with the hope of eternal life.

JAMES 1:2-4 (NIV)

Consider it pure joy, my brothers and sisters, whenever you face trials of many kinds, because you know that the testing of your faith produces perseverance. Let perseverance finish its work so that you may be mature and complete, not lacking anything.

JOB 5:17-18 (WEB)

Behold, happy is the man whom God corrects: Therefore do not despise the chastening of the Almighty. For he wounds, and binds up. He injures, and his hands make whole.

ROMANS 5:1-5 (ESV)

Therefore, since we have been justified by faith, we have peace with God through our Lord Jesus Christ. Through him we have also obtained access by faith into this grace in which we stand, and we rejoice in hope of the glory of God. Not only that, but we rejoice in our sufferings, knowing that suffering produces endurance, and endurance produces character, and character produces hope, and hope does not put us to shame, because God's love has been poured into our hearts through the Holy Spirit who has been given to us.

PSALM 8:3-5 (NIV)

When I consider your heavens, the work of your fingers, the moon and the stars, which you have set in place, what is mankind that you are mindful of them, human beings that you care for them? You have made them a little lower than the angels and crowned them with glory and honor.

EPHESIANS 2:8 (ESV)

For by grace you have been saved through faith. And this is not your own doing; it is the gift of God.

HEBREWS 13:5 (NKJV)

Let your conduct *be* without covetousness; *be* content with such things as you have. For He Himself has said, "I will never leave you nor forsake you."

PSALM 139:13-16 (HCSB)

For it was You who created my inward parts; You knit me together in my mother's womb. I will praise You because I have been remarkably and wonderfully made. Your works are wonderful, and I know this very well. My bones were not hidden from You when I was made in secret, when I was formed in the depths of the earth. Your eyes saw me when I was formless; all my days were written in Your book and planned before a single one of them began.

2 CORINTHIANS 4:15 (ESV)

For it is all for your sake, so that as grace extends to more and more people it may increase thanksgiving, to the glory of God.

1 CHRONICLES 29:13-14 (NIV)

Now, our God, we give you thanks, and praise your glorious name. But who am I, and who are my people, that we should be able to give as generously as this? Everything comes from you, and we have given you only what comes from your hand.

COLOSSIANS 4:2 (AMP)

Be earnest *and* unwearied *and* steadfast in your prayer [life], being [both] alert *and* intent in [your praying] with thanksgiving.

1 THESSALONIANS 5:18 (NLT)

Be thankful in all circumstances, for this is God's will for you who belong to Christ Jesus.

Prepare

Read 1 Chronicles 29:1-20 and then answer the following questions:

Why is King David thankful? How does he give thanks to God?

Are you as passionate as King David about the need to give thanks to God?

Do the people of Israel give thanks to God because they are told to or because they want to? Why is it important to give thanks to God willingly?

How do you show God that you are thankful for His blessings? Do you give thanks willingly to God?

Perform

Make time each day to reflect on all you have to be thankful for. Remind yourself, all that you have has been given to you by God. Seek ways to use the gifts God has given you to live a full life—a life of service to God. Go beyond doing deeds for yourself and others. Give your best each day to God as a way of acknowledging how thankful you are for all He has given you.

> **Song for Reflection:** *Do Everything* by Steven Curtis Chapman
> *Available to watch and listen at **www.youtube.com**.*

Just For Fun

The word *Eucharist* comes from the Greek word *eucharisto*, which means "to give thanks." How many different ways can you say "thank you"? See if you can provide translations for the languages listed below.

Croatian: _____

French: _____

German: _____

Hawaiian: _____

Italian: _____

Japanese: _____

Norwegian: _____

Portuguese: _____

Spanish: _____

Swahili: _____

Closing Thoughts

Each day begins with a simple choice: Will you walk with God today, or will you choose to walk alone?

God never intended for you to be on your own, but He has given you the precious gift of freewill and will not force any choice upon you. If you want to walk with God, this is a choice that you must make.

There may be many days when you do not feel worthy to walk with God. You may feel consumed by failures and the consequences of mistakes you have made. You may be overwhelmed by your own imperfections and sense of inadequacy. You may even think, "How could God love me?"

The good news is that God is fully aware of who you are and all that you have done or have failed to do, and He loves you deeply!

Nothing can separate you from the love of God. He is ready to walk with you if you will allow Him. He will be with you during the most joyful occasions, sharing in your joy and helping you to magnify His presence in this world. He will also be with you during your most difficult moments, helping you to move forward when you are not sure that you have the strength to carry on.

Choosing to walk with God does not mean choosing to be perfect—only God is perfect. Choosing to walk with God means allowing God to guide you to an eternal life with Him. This path cannot be traveled alone. Along the way, there will be many course corrections. You must trust God to lead the way. He will always set you back on the right path if you seek His guidance with an open mind and a willing heart.

Apart from God, each of us is broken and incomplete. We are born into this world with an emptiness that only God can fill. You may find temporary satisfaction and fulfillment if you rely on yourself, but ultimately you must look beyond yourself. God has bigger plans for you than you can ever imagine. You have a loving and caring God who has sacrificed His son so that you might be saved. You are precious in His eyes.

God knows you even better than you know yourself. There is nothing that can be hidden. There is nothing to fear. God will always love you, and His plan is for you to share in His love. He made this possible through His son, Jesus, who is your invitation to an eternity in His loving presence. God makes no demands of you but simply leaves you with a choice: *Will you walk with Him?*

All that is required of you is to place your trust in Him and to live in His Word.

How can a young person stay on the path of purity?
  By living according to your word.

Psalm 119:9 (NIV)

Closing Prayer

Lord, help me to draw closer to you each day—
in my thoughts, in my prayers,
by my actions, and through my words.

Help me to increase in my faith and overcome my fears;
Fill my heart with your love,
and fill my mind with your wisdom.

Lead me to those who are lost, broken, and afraid;
Move my spirit to act with your love and compassion,
and give me your words to speak.

Walk with me Lord,
and help me to see this world with your eyes;
If ever I should stray from you—

      set my feet back on the path to righteousness,
      forgive me of my transgressions,
      and lead me back to you.

Appendix: Just for Fun Answers

Chapter 1:

Bible Verses

And now these three remain: faith, hope and love. But the greatest of these is love. (1 Corinthians 13:13; NIV)

Hatred stirs up conflict, but love covers over all wrongs. (Proverbs 10:12; NIV)

Many waters cannot quench love; rivers cannot wash it away. If one were to give all the wealth of one's house for love, it would be utterly scorned. (Song of Songs 8:7; NIV)

From Movies

To love another person is to see the face of God. (Jean Valjean in *Les Misérables*)

The best love is the kind that awakens the soul and makes us reach for more, that plants a fire in our hearts and brings peace to our minds. (Young Noah in *The Notebook*)

Death cannot stop true love. All it can do is delay it for a while. (Westley in *The Princess Bride*)

Chapter 2:

I lost my wealth, family, and health, but after acknowledging my limitations and placing my trust in God, all was restored to me and I prospered.

(Answer: Job)

I was sold into slavery by my brothers, but I never lost faith in God. I was reunited with my brothers and saved them from suffering during a famine.

(Answer: Joseph)

Our brother became sick and died, but when we sent word to Jesus and asked for His help, He raised our brother from the dead.

(Answer: Martha and Mary)

When confronted by many enemies, I placed my trust in God and He helped me to lead the people of Israel to the Promised Land.

(Answer: Joshua)

Because I refused to stop praying to God, I was thrown to the lions, but God sent an angel to protect me.

(Answer: Daniel)

Chapter 3:

I was a tax collector named Levi when Jesus came and asked me to follow Him.

(Answer: Matthew)

We were with Jesus on the mountain and witnessed His transfiguration.

(Answer: Peter, James, and John)

When Jesus came to me on the road to Damascus, I was temporarily blinded.

(Answer: Saul/Paul)

I am Peter's brother and was fishing with him on the Sea of Galilee when Jesus asked us to become fishers of men.

(Answer: Andrew)

The words *Zealot* and *Canaanite* have been used often to describe me.

(Answer: Simon)

I was chosen as the apostle to replace Judas.

(Answer: Matthias)

I was filled with doubt when Jesus first appeared following His resurrection.

(Answer: Thomas)

Chapter 4:

<u>Priests:</u>

Aaron (also a prophet), Eleazor, Melchizedek (also a king), Zadok

<u>Prophets:</u>

Aaron (also a priest), Anna, Deborah, Ezekiel, Jeremiah, John the Baptist, Malachi, Miriam, Moses, Nathan, Samuel

<u>Kings:</u>

Asa, David, Jehoiakim, Jehoshaphat, Melchizedek (also a priest), Saul, Solomon

Chapter 5:

"Behold, *the* days are coming," says the LORD, "That I will raise to David a Branch of righteousness; A King shall reign and prosper, And execute judgment and righteousness in the earth."

Jeremiah 23:5 (NKJV)

Therefore the Lord himself will give you a sign. Behold, the virgin shall conceive and bear a son, and shall call his name Immanuel.

Isaiah 7:14 (ESV)

But you, Bethlehem Ephrathah, ... out of you shall come forth to Me The One to be Ruler in Israel, Whose goings forth *are* from of old, From everlasting.

Micah 5:2 (NKJV)

And the Son of Man will be delivered over to the chief priests and scribes, and they will condemn him to death and deliver him over to the Gentiles to be mocked and flogged and crucified, and he will be raised on the third day.

Matthew 20:18-19 (ESV)

Chapter 6:

In what three languages was the Bible originally written?

(Answer: Hebrew, Aramaic, and Greek)

Which books in the Bible are referred to as the Pentateuch?

(Answer: Genesis, Exodus, Leviticus, Numbers, and Deuteronomy)

How many verses are in the shortest chapter of the Bible?

(Answer: There are two verses in Psalm 117.)

What is the first book of the New Testament?

(Answer: Matthew)

Which Gospels are referred to as the synoptic Gospels?

(Answer: Matthew, Mark, and Luke)

In which book of the Bible will you find the story of David and Goliath?

(Answer: 1 Samuel)

What are the city names of the seven churches mentioned in the Book of Revelation?

(Answer: Ephesus, Smyrna, Pergamum, Thyatira, Sardis, Philadelphia, and Laodicea)

Chapter 7:

Croatian: *hvala*

French: *merci*

German: *danke*

Hawaiian: *mahalo*

Italian: *grazie*

Japanese: *arigatô*

Norwegian: *takk*

Portuguese: *obrigado; obrigada*

Spanish: *gracias*

Swahili: *asante*

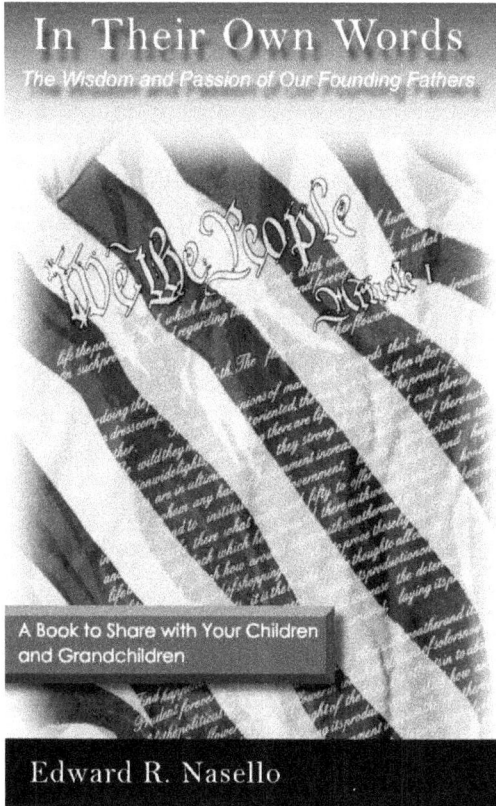

In Their Own Words
The Wisdom and Passion of Our Founding Fathers

We the People

A Book to Share with Your Children
and Grandchildren

Edward R. Nasello

Through the words of our Founding Fathers,
explore their inspired vision for a Godly
nation. *In Their Own Words: The Wisdom and
Passion of Our Founding Fathers* is the perfect
book to read as a family.

www.ingramcontent.com/pod-product-compliance
Lightning Source LLC
Chambersburg PA
CBHW070106070426
42448CB00038B/1834